INTERVIEW WELL AND GET THE JOB

How To Make Finding Work Less Work!

Salim Shaikh

www.smartlyte.co.uk

Birmingham, West Midlands

Copyright © 2015 by Salim Shaikh

All rights reserved. No part of this publication may be reproduced, distributed or transmitted in any form or by any means, including photocopying, recording, or other electronic or mechanical methods, without the prior written permission of the publisher, except in the case of brief quotations embodied in critical reviews and certain other noncommercial uses permitted by copyright law.

Smartlyte Limited
Registered office :
253 Alcester Road South
Kings Heath
Birmingham, UK
B14 6DT

Registered in England & Wales
Company Number: 04965540

Publisher's Note: This book is designed to provide information on the titled topic based on someone else's ideas. This information is provided and sold with the knowledge that the publisher and author do not offer any legal or other professional advice. This information is provided for novelty purposes only. In the case of a need for any such expertise consult with the appropriate professional. This book does not contain all information available on the subject. This book has not been created to be specific to any individual's or organisations' situation or needs. Every effort has been made to make this book as accurate as possible. However, there may be typographical and or content errors. Therefore, this book should serve only as a general guide and not as the ultimate source of subject information. This book contains information that might be dated and is intended only to educate and entertain. The author and publisher shall have no liability or responsibility to any person or entity regarding any loss or damage incurred, or alleged to have incurred, directly or indirectly, by the information contained in this book. You hereby agree to be bound by this disclaimer or you may return this book within the guarantee time period for a full refund.

INTERVIEW WELL AND GET THE JOB. -- 1st ed.

ISBN-13:9781512134568
ISBN-10:1512134562

Special Dedication

FOR MY WIFE;

for encouraging me to believe that everything is possible.

FOR MY CHILDREN;

for believing that everything is possible.

"One important key to success is self-confidence. An important key to self-confidence is preparation."

–Arthur Ashe

CONTENTS

INTRODUCTION i

SECRET TIPS TO INTERVIEW WELL WHEN YOU DESPERATELY WANT THE POSITION YOU HAVE BEEN DESIRING MOST 1

    Practice 2

    Research 2

    Stay calm 3

    Show what you know 3

    Be concise and honest 4

    Confidence 5

    Follow up 6

    Conclusion 6

NINE TOUGH INTERVIEW QUESTIONS AND NINE GREAT RESPONSES YOU MUST KNOW TO ACE THE INTERVIEW 7

    Tell me about yourself? 7

    Why should I hire you? 8

    Are you the best candidate for the job? 9

    What interests you most about this job? 9

    Are you a team player? 10

    Have you ever had a conflict with your boss? How was it resolved? 11

    What are some of your weaknesses? 12

    If given the position, what would you do in your first 90 days? 14

What one particular thing would you change if you had to live your life over again?..15

What Salary range do you expect?..15

HOW TO GET HIRED DURING AN INTERVIEW, PLUS A BONUS SECTION ON HOW TO HANDLE EMPLOYMENT GAPS IN YOUR CURRICULUM VITAE. 17

An important analogy..17

How to get over anxiety..18

Why do you think you will not succeed at a job interview? 19

What do you need to do to prepare for the interview?.......20

How to make a good impression during the interview?....21

How else can you boost your confidence?.........................22

Handling unemployment gaps in your CV.........................22

Chapter Conclusion...23

HOW TO ANSWER ALMOST ANY QUESTION DURING A JOB INTERVIEW..25

Why you should learn how to answer questions during a job interview?...25

Why it is important to answer interview questions effectively..26

What you need to know first before using this technique .26

What to know before going for an interview.....................27

How to answer questions during a job interview?.............27

Chapter conclusion..29

COMMON SENSE ADVICE MOST PEOPLE FORGET WHEN INTERVIEWING - DO NOT FORGET THIS CHAPTER!..31

Why you should prepare thoroughly for a job interview?.32

What you need to know first in order to nail the job interview? 32

How to handle yourself on the day of the interview? 34

Chapter conclusion 36

THE LESSONS INTERVIEWERS ARE TAUGHT THAT YOU SHOULD KNOW AND HOW THEY SPOT LIARS FAST 37

Being the interviewer for a time 37

How you'll know that your interviewee is lying 39

Final note 39

TOP SECRET NLP SECRETS FOR ACING THE INTERVIEW EVERYTIME 41

Get the most out of your interviewer: 42

NLP techniques to help you ace the interview 43

Matching and Mirroring 43

Pacing and Leading 46

Anchoring 47

Chapter conclusion 49

AUTHOR'S FINAL NOTES 51

References 55

About The Author 61

INTRODUCTION

Thank you for purchasing this book.

Perhaps you've wondered why some people have no problem getting a job, whilst others watch with envy, wishing they could just as easily get hired in a position of their choosing? It is frustrating, isn't it? I mean, watching someone you know get a job—like it's nothing—while you can't seem to get a break.

What about the unemployed jobseeker? What about the parents who have been out of work for a period—possibly years? How are they hired? Especially given there are so many other candidates who seem far more likely to be chosen. What is really the secret to getting back up on the horse and ending joblessness, so you can truly achieve the lifestyle dreams you have in mind? Believe it or not, trying to get back into the workforce after an extended period of joblessness is much like going on a blind-date with someone you have never met before. Fear overcomes you. You start to stress out. You find yourself failing before you have even begun. Let us be honest, it is scary, isn't it? Many times people have reported to me that they've even been depressed as they have gone about trying to get a job due to how challenging they found it. Perhaps you can relate to this yourself.

Being unemployed can result in a stressful mental trap. While it is a period of immense strain, being depressed only makes it that much more difficult to get back to work. Before we begin this journey of achieving desired work, I want to explain a few of the issues faced by jobseekers and methods to tackle them. What are the barriers faced by unemployed people?

Of the many obstacles surrounding the world, unemployment is one of the hardest to face because life becomes a list of compromises and sacrifices. Here are a few of the most common problems that come with being unemployed.

Low Finances: The initial setback is the plummeting finances that drastically reduce the security in a household. To combat this, immediate steps need to be taken to reduce expenditure on anything that is not absolutely necessary for day to day living.

Mounting Pressure: As the days turn to weeks, stress builds up immensely, leaving a person feeling frustrated. It is essential to understand that being jobless can be just a phase that can eventually pass. Staying calm is essential.

Finding Work: It isn't as easy finding a job as it is losing one. For this reason it is important to find the right job. The right job means discovering where you fit in, then pursuing that, and only that. Without the right fit you'll be unhappy, and you'll only be working to support yourself, and be assured it will be more challenging finding work, once you are already gainfully employed somewhere else. The reason for this is because you'll be working somewhere where you don't fit in, and you'll not have the time to dedicate to finding something else. Many people settle into a job accepting it as their lot in life. This can be problematic. It is better to pursue the right career path as soon as you can, as you'll be more satisfied, do better work, and your health and well-being will be better too. For this reason you must investigate, ask yourself questions, and decide what type of work fits you best.

Low Confidence Levels: For many, the automatic reaction to losing a job is self-deprecation and helplessness. Having a negative attitude may impact prospective interviews. To battle stress, people need to try and keep themselves engaged in the activity of finding work; that is, be proactive.

While it may be difficult, it's important to remain composed and optimistic in the face of unemployment. Just remember that life is full of ups and downs. If you are at the bottom already, there is nowhere else to go but up again. A positive outlook is the path to finding the solution.

You see; the truth of the matter is we have all had issues finding a job at one time or another in our lives. I have found, through my work and having interviewed thousands of job candidates, that there are some patterns which emerge, which, when studied, can actually predict who will get a job, and who will not. I know this sounds a bit far-fetched. Do not think of it this way though. Think about the implications of what I am actually eliciting for just a moment. To do this, let us look at a different context altogether:

Imagine back to childhood, when you were in primary school. Remember the children who seemed to be the most popular? Perhaps this might have been you. Maybe it was not. In either case, you probably noticed some people have a certain charisma about them, a likability factor if you will, that sets them apart from the majority of others. When people are interviewing for an opportunity to work for a company of their choosing, the interviewer is seeking a particular calibre. This calibre is a metric by which a pile of CVs filters down until the best candidate is determined and offered the position.

When you think about it like this, you probably consider that your chances of getting a job you want are slim to none at best. It does not really have to be this way though. You see, all you have to do in order to get the position is make yourself the best candidate out of that list. You have to make it obvious that you will excel the best in that position. Convincing yourself of this is not necessary. Convincing the person interviewing you is what is most critical.

If you're like me, you've probably psyched yourself up to feel more confident and qualified to do something you wanted to do, but which you almost certainly had second thoughts you could in fact accomplish. There is a nervous anxiety that befalls those individuals who probably will not be getting the position when they actually go in for the interview. I learnt from previous experience early on in life, that I always got a sense of anxiousness that prevented me from being the best candidate even when I should have been. If you have worked in fast food your whole life, and going in for a job as a fast food employee, then chances are you're well qualified and would be a shoe in, but this does not necessarily mean you will be the person getting the job. You have to differentiate yourself from the competition. You have to be unforgettable. You have to believe you are the best candidate.

In this book, you're going to discover how to actually be the best candidate. You're going to learn that everything begins and ends with communication. As such, you're going to learn some highly covert and secretive communication techniques. Sure, you'll learn the basics, because it's important to know these things, and to be refreshed on them as well, and this book of course wouldn't be complete without them. However, you'll as well be learning things you've never learned anywhere else before, most likely. This is because many are never exposed to this type of information. So if you're picking up this book, pat yourself on the back now, because you're in for a ride. You're in for a journey that will not only excite you, but by the time you finish reading this book, you'll know well enough that you've got that job you've been wanting. You will also know that you have what it takes to ace the interview.

With all this being said I want to thank you for picking up a copy of this book, and when you're finished with it, and you've gotten a dream job that you've always wanted; I invite you to take a few minutes to email us and let us know of your success story. It's important to us to get your feedback. And, if you're willing to, we'd love to stay in touch.

CHAPTER 1

SECRET TIPS TO INTERVIEW WELL WHEN YOU DESPERATELY WANT THE POSITION YOU HAVE BEEN DESIRING MOST

Job interviewing is never easy, even for those who have gone to more interviews than they can count. You are always having to sell yourself and sometimes it is not easy selling to perfect strangers in a job interview. The challenge is to stay enthusiastic and upbeat throughout each interview. The key to a successful interview is keeping anxiety under control to manage the level of stress. Proper preparation will always be a good help in alleviating job interview stress as well as contributing to your confidence pool.

Here are secret job interview tips -learn these and you'll start off on the right track for sure:

Practice

Review some common interview questions and practice answering them with a friend or in front of a mirror. Think of concrete examples you can use to demonstrate how skillful you are. To promote your candidacy, provide evidence of your successes.

Figure out how well you qualify for the job in advance. Consider which skills you possess and which skills you lack. This can be done by assessing yourself against the job description and person specification. This will help you plan how to address this in the interview and convince the interviewer that you are able to learn the skill. Be prepared with a list of your own questions to ask the interviewer when the chance presents itself. Let the question demonstrate that you've researched the company and are informed about the job role on offer.

Research

Make sure that you are ready to answer the question "What do you know about this company?" Research the interviewer's name and make sure that you know their job title and position within the company. Conduct thorough research on the company's salary scale. How large is it? What will be your role? Have there been any recent changes made in the company?

This will enable you to identify if this is the right job for you, therefore, you will be confident while approaching the interview room. Sometimes just having an inner-knowing that you are partnering with the right company, before the interview begins, will give you a confidence boost and help you secure the position for yourself. Some people report, "I just had a feeling the job was mine (!)," after following this advice.

Stay calm

Relaxing and staying calm during the interview helps you to maintain your confidence. You should remember that your body language says so much about you. Proper preparations will allow you to display confidence. Maintain eye contact with the interviewer and engage in active listening to avoid embarrassment should you forget the question.

Show what you know

When answering questions try to relate them with what you know about the company. Match your career accomplishments with what the company is looking for. Present your achievements to the interviewer in a manner suggesting you know what they need, and you know you are the solution. Great sales professionals understand this problem-solution approach to winning over prospects and converting them into buyers.

Be concise and honest

Listening actively is not enough unless you add the concept of answering concisely. Stick to the question asked and give fine informed details. Lack of preparation and research makes interviewees divert from the question asked and deliver verbose or vague answers. Overstating and talking too much is a characteristic of someone ill prepared, nervous, and lacking in self-confidence. Do not do it.

Dancing around difficult interview questions is not a solution either. If you do not have a skill, then just open up. Never try to cover-up by talking too much and giving irrelevant examples. Honesty is a good quality and demonstrating it can earn you more points. Keep in mind always: Whenever you are faced with a question asking you to choose between two stances, always choose honesty over any other choice. Interviewers are trained to take note of this during interviews. If you leave honesty behind, you could jeopardise your chances of getting selected.

Confidence

This is the most important quality you need in order to be successful at an interview. This does not mean you should not come into the interview as the best candidate with the right skill set. However, without confidence, all other tips will be useless. Showing confidence creates a great first impression in the interview room. It gives you the self-belief to think normally and digest interview questions in the proper manner. It also helps you to remember all that you researched. To show that you are confident sends a positive message with your body language. To demonstrate that you are confident you should:

1. Maintain eye contact

2. Shake hands firmly

3. Ask for clarification or repetition if you did not understand a question

4. Be honest and give direct answers

5. End with a lasting good impression on the interviewer

A positive end is another way of ensuring interview success. Be courteous and allow the interview to end in good time. You can recap any experience and strength that you may not have had the opportunity to emphasise earlier. Ask the interviewer when he or she intends to make a decision, how they will inform you and find out if there will be additional interviews.

Follow up

Following up with a thank you note is very important. You can use this opportunity to include some details which you could have left out or forgotten to mention during the interview. If you were interviewed by a panel of several people, send each one a personal thank you note. It's always better if you send it within 24 hours of your interview

Conclusion

Interviews can be a nightmare, especially if it is your first one. Proper preparation and confidence can transform the nightmare into a sweet dream. Always make sure you follow this invaluable advice and the job will be more yours.

CHAPTER 2

NINE TOUGH INTERVIEW QUESTIONS AND NINE GREAT RESPONSES YOU MUST KNOW TO ACE THE INTERVIEW

The best way to prepare for an interview is to come up with questions you think are likely to be asked, and then come up with answers ahead of time. This chapter will focus on some of the most difficult questions you will likely come across during a job interview and how you should answer them.

Tell me about yourself?

This looks like a very easy interview question. One can talk about whatever he or she wants from birth to the present day, right? Wrong! What the interviewer wants is a two to three minute answer of who you are and why you are the right candidate for the position.

For this reason, when you are answering this question, try to talk about your work experience such that you position yourself as the best candidate for the job. It is advisable to support your answer with two or three examples. Ask if you should give more details. If the interviewer says yes, continue giving more examples of your experience and background.

"Tell me about yourself" does not entail talking about just anything you want to share about your personal life - say what makes you the best candidate.

Why should I hire you?

The best answer to this question is that you are the right person for the job. Do not be afraid to say so, but support your answer with what precisely makes you the best person for the job.

For example, "The main reason you should hire me is because I'm the right person for the job. I know there are other candidates who can effectively do this job. However, I bring additional qualities that will make me the best person for this specific position you have available. I have excellent oral and written communication skills. I am a team player, self-driven, focused and hard working. I will always keep improving and adding value to the company. This is why you should hire me."

Are you the best candidate for the job?

When asked as a follow-up question, "Are you the best candidate for the job?" Answer this question using your passionate examples. This means knowing these ahead of time, before the interview ever starts. Passion is an attribute associated with high-achievers; meaning, you want the interviewer to recognise this about you.

What interests you most about this job?

This is a tricky question; as a result, do not talk about things that are unrelated to the day to day work. It will show you are not enthusiastic about the job itself. For example, do not talk about salary, benefits or the short commute. Interviewers are mostly looking at what you offer and not what the job can do for you. Talk about your passion for this job, and the skills you are going to bring.

Are you a team player?

Most people usually say yes to this question. This is not just a yes or no question. You need to back up your answer with behavioural or competency based examples.

For example, "Yes, I am a team player. My skills as a team player developed a lot when I had opportunities at work, athletics or school. For instance, on a recent project..." and complete your story. Great sales professionals know the power of telling stories. They say:

"Stories sell; facts fail!"

Talk about your strength as a team player, but remember that this question may lead to other questions. For example, how did you handle conflict within a team? Therefore, be prepared and pay special attention to these presupposition-questions. Recognise that there may be traps used against you to learn more about you; namely, things you do not want to reveal during the interview.

Have you ever had a conflict with your boss? How was it resolved?

If your answer is no, note that the majority of interviewers will drill deeper to find a conflict. The interviewer just wants to know how you react to conflict and how you resolve it.

For example, "Yes, there have been conflicts with my boss in the past. However, they were not major conflicts and they were just typically small disagreements which were easily resolved. I find most conflicts revolve around missing information, distorted facts, or over generalisations. Using empathy and my strong communication skills make it possible to resolve conflict and reach a resolution. One thing I have noted about conflicts, are that they enable one to understand the other person's perspective. So I usually take time to listen to the other person's point of view, and then come up with a collaborative solution."

Your answer should revolve around behavioural process and working as a team to come up with a solution. Nothing is ever one sided.

What are some of your weaknesses?

Most career advisors will tell you to come up with a strength and present it as a weakness. For example, "I guess I'm a workaholic, but I really love to work." Wrong! Using your strength and presenting it as a weakness is very deceiving because it misses the central point of the question. You should only take this approach, in my professional opinion, if you talk about a weakness that has some merit. For instance;

"One weakness I have is micromanaging every detail of a project. I suppose this is because my tendency is to take ownership of the project. However, I am recognising more and more that the project is a team effort, and therefore I must trust more in the process of teamwork.

"In the past, when I have worked in teams, I have generally been informally designated the team leader. I enjoy responsibility but I recognise I do need to hold others more accountable for their roles."

Notice this is a strength converted into a weakness; yet done so tastefully and in a way to which others will relate. Interviewers will be able to relate to such a response, as most people find themselves in similar circumstances throughout their professional life.

Another way to answer this question is only select a weakness you have been genuinely working hard to overcome. For example, "I have had challenges in the past when it came to planning and prioritisation, however, I am working to overcome this. Actually, I just purchased a pocket planner..." go on to show the interviewer how your pocket planner is helping you to overcome your weakness. This type of answer shows integrity; however, it also depicts your ability to problem solve, i.e. a strength.

Both ways work, because the first capitalises on taking a strength and turning it into a weakness, and in the second instance, you are taking a weakness and turning it into a strength. Either approach will distract the interviewer away from your weakness, and help you bring out your strengths. Remember, this question is an opportunity to share your strengths, not your weaknesses. Even so it is still better to pick a weaker area and simply admit you need some improvement in this area. This shows integrity and that you're human. Interviewers will appreciate you not being cliché in how you answer, too.

If given the position, what would you do in your first 90 days?

In this situation, the interviewer just wants to know how you set goals. Are your goals realistic? How will you solve problems? Tell the interviewer you would like to meet the rest of the team so you can know the company's needs before making any significant decisions. Then share how you set-goals and achieve results. Whenever possible, ask for more information from the interviewer about the role and what is typical in terms of problems that surface. This will not only show you care, it will give you an opportunity to learn more about the company and what role you will be playing in it. It also gives you a rest from answering questions as the interviewer will be the one doing the talking for a time. Unbelievably, most interviewers would rather be sharing information with you, not extracting it from you. Ask yourself this question, "Who do people care more about - themselves or others? Most people would rather be doing the talking while someone else listens. This is a powerful thing to keep in mind.

What one particular thing would you change if you had to live your life over again?

Talk about any missed opportunity or turning point in your life.

For example, "Presently I'm happy with where I am in my life. The one thing I would have loved to change would have been to focus earlier on the direction of my career. Last year I had a great year, and I look forward to gaining more experience in the field. For instance, I learned a lot about ___ (fill in the blank). Then give more examples. Remember, these stories sell the interviewer on you and make you unforgettable in their mind.

Your answers should focus more on the positive direction, and support it using examples.

What Salary range do you expect?

This is a surprisingly common question. Be confident in your answer – it should be based on prior research hooked on salary averages for the industry and job role. Advise a figure that's a little bit higher than the average. Do this because you should not undersell yourself and you could end up earning a bit more than average. Do not ask for too much- most companies have a budget they have to maintain, and you don't want them to consider your services unaffordable. Be affordable, but not underpaid.

You can even say, "My experience and research show me that people in this position generally earn somewhere in between £20,000 and £30,000 annually. However, there are a number of things to consider, for example, career progression and development, the people I will be working with and, of course, the job itself."

An interview is your only chance of making a good first impression to your potential employer. If you prepare well for an interview, you will have the confidence that will earn you that dream job. Always respond with information that shows you are the best person for the job.

Remember, the above responses are only examples. It is not advisable to rehearse them for use in an interview. They are meant to help you in your creativity and the range of questions you will be asked.

CHAPTER 3

HOW TO GET HIRED DURING AN INTERVIEW, PLUS A BONUS SECTION ON HOW TO HANDLE EMPLOYMENT GAPS IN YOUR CURRICULUM VITAE.

Have you ever thought of a scenario where you walk into an interview and sail through it without hitting any bumps? Did you ever think that this was just an impossible scene for you? Because if your answer is yes, then you are actually wrong! Succeeding in an interview is a feat that you can definitely accomplish. All you have to do is learn some of the basic knowhow and reflect on some questions mentioned in this chapter to help you achieve your goals.

An important analogy

An interview is often a nerve-wracking experience, much like a blind date can be. The element of uncertainty is what creates the sense of insecurity that can cause you to perform poorly. You need to know how to get rid of that fear effectively.

How to get over anxiety

Here are a few tips you can follow to get rid of your trepidation and become better at handling sudden situations:

Embrace the Unknown

When you are presented with a situation where you don't know what to expect, consider it a challenge and be prepared for both the best case and the worst case scenarios.

Be Spontaneous

Unknown situations provide people with a chance to showcase their natural ability. There is more of an element of truth in rising to the occasion instantly than there is in planned responses.

Be Prepared

Understand that both success and failure are possible, but being prepared gives you a higher chance of succeeding and will automatically make you more calm and composed.

Portray Confidence

Confidence is the most attractive quality a person can have, be it as a new employee or on a first date. It creates an excellent first impression before you even get started.

Be Natural

Being in strange and uncomfortable situations can force people to put on an artificial attitude but that will only make matters worse. You must remember that it is more important to be liked for who you are than for who you pretend to be.

Most things in life carry no certainty and this includes jobs and relationships. The only thing you can be certain about is that you are willing to try your best and walk out with your dignity intact. Follow these tips and pretty soon you will have an offer letter in hand and a second date planned within no time! Now let us look at some more questions you should be aware of.

Why do you think you will not succeed at a job interview?

This is a challenging question to answer—perhaps the hardest! The reason is that while answering it, you will have to be honest with yourself. Many people have fear of success simply because they do not know how it is going to change their lives. If you realise that this is your problem, just break up the situation into tiny piecemeal portions which you can manage easily. In addition, you may realise that part of your fear may result from the theoretical 'what-ifs'. What if your interviewer asks you a question and you cannot answer? What will happen if you do not get the job? All these hypothetical 'what-ifs' will stop you from achieving what you want namely, the job. It is important not to over think too much and to go in somewhat clear and expectant and you'll get the job. This change of mindset will benefit you immeasurably during the interview, but also in other areas of your life, such as your new position.

What do you need to do to prepare for the interview?

You can control your time and effort spent in preparing for the interview; make a list to think of all points that you should be covering during your preparation. You can make sure your CV is up to date and focus on the main criteria that the job profile requires. Try to practice your style in delivering speeches perfectly.

How to make a good impression during the interview?

There are some points that you can follow to impress your interviewer so that after the interview is over, they are still thinking of you:

Your voice should be clear with your eyes looking straight ahead at the interviewer. This creates an impression of your honesty and straightforwardness.

Be engaging. Talk about several activities which reflect your strength in playing as a team member. Focus on telling them stories of your success in the previous job positions you have held.

Try to lighten the ambience with humour. Nevertheless, make sure you do not go overboard. Simply keep it light and then immediately move on to the next topic.

Answer with conviction and passion in your voice. Show them that you really care about your work and you identify with it. This will never fail to make a great impression.

How else can you boost your confidence?

Confidence is the key to success here. Do not think of your interview as either a make-it or break-it scenario, think of it as an opportunity. You will automatically start feeling more calm and relaxed, which will help you to answer questions confidently and precisely.

Handling unemployment gaps in your CV.

Unemployment is a challenge to many job seekers today because of the limited job vacancies available for them. Many jobless persons remain unemployed for extended periods and as a result they have large or frequent unemployment gaps. However, unemployment gaps on a CV can be mitigated if the below advice is followed:

1. Use years only to show the dates in your work history.

2. When you use years instead of months to show various job periods it eliminates the months you were jobless, and the integrity of your CV will be maintained.

3. Ensure that you include all voluntary activities where you worked.

4. Any volunteering, internship, training or family activities that you undertake during the unemployment period and which are relevant to the job vacancy should be added to your CV. In addition, you can also include the online jobs, blogging or just state you were working as a freelancer if indeed you have the relevant work samples or websites that you have been using.

If the gaps in the CV were a result of irrelevant work history, be brief and honest when explaining. As human beings we are not infallible; meaning, we are susceptible to getting ill, having some health complications and simply needing time off to take care for aging family members or raising a family. There is nothing wrong with admitting this during an interview. Most interviewers have been in a same or similar situation or knows someone else who has and they will empathise and understand where you're coming from.

Chapter Conclusion

If you follow these instructions carefully you will feel empowered and confident! The only thing you need to do now is to practice these key elements and then produce an awesome interview performance! You will also be able to eliminate gaps in your employment so they satisfy the interviewer. Remember, just like a blind date, having a successful interview is all about the approach. Get self-confidence working for you and you'll be working sooner than your realise. The position will be yours!

CHAPTER 4

HOW TO ANSWER ALMOST ANY QUESTION DURING A JOB INTERVIEW

Have you ever wondered how you are going to answer questions during an interview to guarantee you the job? Well, I am going to teach you how now. You will be astonished at how very simple things will determine whether you get the job or not.

Why you should learn how to answer questions during a job interview?

Learn how to answer questions during an interview and you will become a job seeker no more. This topic is vital because it teaches you a skill fundamental to getting that job you have always dreamed of having. Your chances of getting the job are reduced if you do not come across as a persuasive person. You can persuade the interviewer into recruiting you if you know how to answer the questions correctly during the interview.

Why it is important to answer interview questions effectively.

Learning the important skills and methodologies for answering interview questions is an important way for a jobseeker to demonstrate their suitability for a particular job. Having the right mannerisms, attitude, and eloquence can be vital in making a long lasting impression on the interviewer. This can enhance your prospects of securing the job.

What you need to know first before using this technique

Image matters. You should be aware of this by now. The way you present yourself will speak volumes about who you are. Make sure your hair is neat and your suit is clean and ironed. Be smart and presentable! This will impact how you are judged by the interview panel. Posture is also vital. Sit in a manner that suggests that you know why you have been invited before that panel. Observe etiquette always; these are the conventional forms of social interaction. Always treat people with consideration, respect and honesty. Your actions will always have an effect on you. You never know, maybe the person seated next to you on the train is among the interviewing panel you have an appointment with that afternoon.

Gather information about the company you look forward to working with.

What to know before going for an interview

Giving the right impression to interviewers is essential for succeeding in an interview. This means employing all manner of tactics such as charm, eloquence, dressing, tone, clarity of voice, among other pertinent factors. All these factors are esteem for providing an image that seems appealing, focused, and intelligent to the interviewer.

How to answer questions during a job interview?

Do the following and you can't go wrong:

1. Say as many positive things about the company as possible.

2. Never say "No" to "Have you done this type of work before?" question. Stress any experience you have that will help you learn faster and work more efficiently.

3. State your best qualifications for the job. Be specific and site examples to show the employer you meet their expectations.

4. Stick to active hobbies, such as playing sports, gardening etc. Avoid mentioning inactive hobbies like watching television.

5. If any, describe volunteer work you do whether it is related to the work you are being interviewed for or not. It is common knowledge that people who donate their time to help others free of charge are doing a worthwhile thing by developing their skills and experiences. Employers like this quality in an applicant.

6. Be positive about yourself and your previous employer.

7. Turn your weaknesses into strengths that work to the advantage of your employer.

8. Comment on your transferable skills, such as reliable, punctual, organised, responsible, etc.

9. Be honest in a positive way on everything.

10. Do not discuss salary unless the interviewer raises the topic. In such a case, leave the impression you are flexible in this area.

Chapter conclusion

Interviews are avenues through which candidates can display their basic and unique qualifications that make them suitable for a particular job. Answering questions in the interview requires careful and articulate answers that promote an image of intelligence and strong interpersonal skills to increase a candidate's suitability for the job.

Firstly, make sure prior to answering a question that you fully understand its content. This means that the candidate should seek clarification for questions they did not hear or understand. Additionally, they should stop and think critically about the question asked and answer it in a manner that the interviewer expects.

Secondly, the candidate should refresh their knowledge in their field of study in case any related questions are asked. This may simply be reading through your CV just before the interview. This helps you to refresh your knowledge and contents of your CV and you will be able to answer any questions that the interviewer may ask you in relation to this. You will sound more confident and honest as your answer will reinforce the information that you have on your CV.

Finally, the candidate should answer questions in short, precise and articulate answers that do not veer off into unrelated areas. Providing long answers usually results in the candidate giving too much information that could be irrelevant and could bore the interviewers. This has the negative effect of interviewers deeming the candidate as lacking judgment.

This lesson has provided you with a very useful skill set that will come in handy during your next interview. You are now able to properly prepare yourself for an interview and tackle interview questions with accuracy and confidence. Congratulations on your new job.

CHAPTER 5

COMMON SENSE ADVICE MOST PEOPLE FORGET WHEN INTERVIEWING - DO NOT FORGET THIS CHAPTER!

Have you ever asked yourself what valid reason you have not to give a good interview? Sometimes simply answering this question will give you the motivation to pull forward and be more self-confident and interview again and again until you get the job you dream of having. Make yourself ready to tackle any questions that may come up during the job interview. The information outlined in this chapter explores common forgotten etiquette and necessary points of reference that must be followed in every job interview. After you finish with this chapter, you ought to have a fairly substantial understanding of how to interview. Really, it is common sense advice, but it is advise people more often than not forget during an interview.

Why you should prepare thoroughly for a job interview?

Prepare thoroughly to be successful in a job interview. The guidelines are very important because they give insight on the kind of questions and challenges you are likely to face during the interview. If you prepare for the type of interview in advance, you'll be better prepared to make a proper presentation of your skill set. Rehearsing ahead of time is a great idea, as when you get into the interview room, you'll be more focused and ready to give a proper introduction of yourself. Good interview preparation gives you massive advantages over the other interviewees and raises your chances of securing the job opportunity.

What you need to know first in order to nail the job interview?

Make yourself ready. There is a list of things you should be aware of before attending any job interview. These things include:

1. Knowledge of the organisation and the job. First, one should be able to research and review the organisation

thoroughly and the details of the job opportunity being offered.

2. Know how well qualified you are for the job. Contemplate how well your experience, interests and abilities fit the occupation and the organisation offering the job.

3. Be educated on the current patterns in the job and the employment sector as well

4. Know what the prospective employer is looking for in a candidate. This will include reviewing the level of experience, interest and the skills associated with the job. This information can be found in the job description and person specification for the position you are being interviewed for.

5. You should be aware of the questions likely to be asked during the interview. Equip yourself with the most appropriate answers for the most common interview questions and others you think are likely to be asked.

6. Be aware of the kind of interview you will be attending. It could be a single interview (this is where you face one individual interviewer), panel interview (this

is where you face a number of interviewers) or group interview (this is where many interviewees are interviewed simultaneously).

How to handle yourself on the day of the interview?

Understand the right way to carry yourself on the day of the interview. This will include the proper dress code, conduct and self-presentation in the interview. With the proper self-handling and self-discipline you are very likely to be awarded the job opportunity. You will discover how easy it is to tackle the job interview when it is done right. We will now have a look at the things that need to be done on the day of the interview:

1. Arrive earlier than the time scheduled for the interview. This will help reflect your reliability to the potential employer. It may also help you to relax before the interview, as you are able to familiarise yourself with the surroundings.

2. Take with you all the necessary documents related to the job opportunity, these should entail a proper written application letter, CV and any other documents

that you may need as indicated during correspondence with the company.

3. Be attentive: during the job interview, you should listen carefully to the questions posed by the interviewer.

4. Be concise in answering questions asked during the interview.

5. Highlight your best characteristics in the meeting. Before you leave, think about what you want the interviewer to think about you (in connection to the job at hand) and state it politely amid the interview session.

6. Consider the way you communicate. In many instances body language is more important than what you actually say, so if you portray yourself as confident make sure your body language reflects this. Do practice answers to what you expect to be asked at the interview before you arrive. This could be through saying the words aloud as it helps build confidence as you hear yourself speak.

7. If you happen to bring your mobile phone to the interview ensure that it is in the silent mode or better yet, switched off.

Chapter conclusion

In this chapter, you learnt a lot about how to excel in the interview. You learnt some dos and don'ts. In the main, you learnt what to be cognizant of and what you must ensure you are prepared for ahead of time. This will ensure you get the job of your dreams and ace every interview in which you find yourself.

CHAPTER 6

THE LESSONS INTERVIEWERS ARE TAUGHT THAT YOU SHOULD KNOW AND HOW THEY SPOT LIARS FAST

This chapter takes a different approach. You will step inside the shoes of the interviewer and understand what they learn when they are learning how to interview. So let us do a little pretending here, and let us suppose instead of being the interviewee, you are the interviewer. Once you know what your interviewer has been trained in, it becomes much easier to plan your interview effectively.

Being the interviewer for a time...

How can you easily discover that a person is lying in a job interview? Do not put yourself in the position of the interviewee, but instead be an interviewer for a moment and discover when you should not do things that will expose you to others. A great interviewer will notice when you are just bluffing them. So, how can you avoid these things in case you interview people for a job? Lying always causes a degree of psychological stress which manifests itself in one's body language. Charles Darwin, who was among the first scientists who studied the emotions, stressed that these kinds of internal conflicts usually float to the surface—represented by body language; namely, which is composed of non-verbal human behaviour elements including facial expressions and the status of the body. Dr. Glenn Wilson, from the Institute of Psychiatry in London, adds that the body language is very important. It is difficult for you to align congruently body language and verbal communication at the same time. Therefore, the non-verbal signals, known as infusions, usually expose a lie. For example, when someone is lying, she or he avoids eye contact, fearing that you (the interviewer) can detect when they are lying or being deceptive.

Most people use their own hands when they speak and they know that these gestures transfer parts of their meanings. Usually the lying person uses fewer gestures of the hands and arms than someone being legitimately honest and forthright does. Therefore, among the signs that may designate someone is lying, we notice characteristics like: (a) putting the hands in the pockets, (b) embracing the palms and (c) putting the hands and fingers inward rather than outward. The only gesture being replicated when lying is shaking shoulders, which is an expression of disapproval or indifference. It is as if the hands want to deny what the mouth says. Moreover, if you are a subtle and careful observer, you may pay attention to the false tension manifesting in the body language of someone who is being deceptive.

How you'll know that your interviewee is lying

1. Sweating: The lying person sweats too much as he/she become nervous and cannot control him/herself.

2. The position of the eyes: When looking to the left side, he is probably lying.

3. The throat: A lying person's throat tends to become dry so he needs to drink or swallow fast.

4. The voice projection: The lying person starts speaking rapidly or slowly and most often raises his voice.

Final note

As you can plainly see, lying is easier to detect than you might have thought previously. Deception is easily detected in body language and verbal mismatching. If you've lied on your

CV, created a hyped-up story behind why you have been a constant job-hopper, or have it in your mind you're going to embellish the truth to make yourself appear like the best candidate—you may want to rethink this strategy. At the very least you want to make sure you are aligning your body language, tone of speech, and what you say congruently so that when you do interview you don't get perceived as a dishonest candidate. The best case scenario is not to lie and still get the job!

I have known many people over the years that have lost wonderful job opportunities simply because they were unable to tell the truth, or at least be perceived as telling the truth. If you have lied about your education credentials, your job history, or even the length of time you worked at your pervious jobs, then be prepared for what your interviewer will likely be on the lookout for when you meet them face to face. It is difficult to hide or mask your unconscious movements. If you are going to lie, you will need to know how to ensure your body language does not reflect that of liars.

CHAPTER 7

TOP SECRET NLP SECRETS FOR ACING THE INTERVIEW EVERYTIME

Have you ever heard of Neuro Linguistic Programming? Do you know how it is used? This chapter will teach you the intricacies of NLP, what it is, and most importantly how to use these techniques while being interviewed for a position you want desperately to get.

NLP is a communication approach devised in 1970 by Richard Bandler and John Grinder. This approach is valid because there is a connection between the thinking process, the language people use and the general behaviour a person has learned. NLP is based on two principles; one is that our perception of reality influences how we speak, behave, and think. The other is that our bodies are systemic with our environment; that is, the environment a person is in dictates how they think, form their words, and how they tend to act. Used as a tool, NLP gauges the emotional quotient of a person. It can help you understand your interviewer just by how they communicate. It can help promote empathy. As an interviewee, there are various basic questions to ask—while you ask, all you need to know and study are the tonal patterns and body language of the interviewer.

Get the most out of your interviewer:

1. Create a rapport with the interviewer. You can do this by leading the conversation using keywords and you can respond to the interviewer's non-verbal cues like their eye movements. For example, if the interviewer is confident about the current topic of discussion he/she will maintain eye contact, take this as a cue and exploit that topic. This will help you maintain rapport.

2. Ask questions that can help you determine the interviewer's current state and his/her future goals with the company. Pay attention to verbal (does the tone show excitement?) and non-verbal cues.

3. Finally, determine if the interviewer is able to cope with any changes the company may have experienced recently. This will help them open up, be more expressive and give more clarity and insight about the

company. It will also prove to them that you are up to date on what has been happening with the company. You can usually get this information by researching the company website for any company announcements or documents like the most recent quarterly report, if this is available.

NLP techniques to help you ace the interview

Going to an interview has never been an easy task. It requires only the strong and successful candidate to make a compelling argument for why they should be hired; usually by explaining how they can solve a problem for the company, no other candidate can. Doing this has never been a walk in the park either. Advanced strategies and techniques are required.

Below are useful NLP techniques that will land you your dream job:

Matching and Mirroring

Matching and mirroring are two techniques used to gain rapport at the unconscious level. Rapport is the foundation of a meaningful interaction between two people. It is about establishing an understanding environment which gives you freedom to fully express your concerns and ideas and where each person respects and appreciates the others' viewpoints. Mirroring is about watching the other person's body language such as hand gestures, postures, facial expression, rate of speech, volume and applying it to your body language.

Generally, people act, look, move and sound like one another, they tend to notice these similarities at the unconscious level, which makes them get along very well with each other. We can therefore gain rapport with any kind of person just by emulating the person by using the process of mirroring and matching.

There are a number of Neuro-linguistic elements you can use to mirror and match a person. You can mirror or match blinking and facial expression, voice, attitude, position, posture, words and gesturing. For example, when a person inclines their head to the right, you should tilt your head to the left, just like in a mirror. When you sit across from someone, assume a mirrored position of your head legs and hands. When a person talks, you can observe the gestures they are using and also their hand movements. Try using the same gestures when responding back but avoid trying to imitate every gesture; else it will look like you are trying to play the monkey game.

A better way to do it is by being discreet while using this technique. You can holdup an action for a few seconds. For example, if a person changes his or her position, match it by shifting after some time.

Crossover mirroring is also another useful technique. In this technique, when a person shifts one part of his or her body, mirror it by shifting some other part of your body. For example, if a person moves his leg, mirror by moving your hand. Breathing can also be matched by moving your finger with the same speed and frequency as that of their breathing. Such techniques help you implement the mirroring and matching technique without the other person being aware of what you're doing.

Establishing good rapport is crucial during an interview; remember people hire people they like. So making the interviewer like you, by making them feel at ease, while conversing with you, might be the difference between getting a job or not.

In an interview, matching and mirroring the verbal and physical styles of the interviewer can determine your success. This is because the technique makes the interviewer more comfortable; thus, enabling them to optimise their ability to hear your message. If your interviewer is not jovial, match his verbal cues with corresponding behaviour and avoid cracking jokes. When seated, make sure that you watch if your interviewer is leaning backward or forward and adjust your posture appropriately.

Pacing and Leading

Pacing means entering into someone's model of the world, match him or her, and fall into step with him. In other words, it is a strategy to take control of a situation. You can pace someone's beliefs, ideas, experiences, words and behaviour. You do not have to share the ideas and beliefs; you just need to fall into step with them just for a while.

Once rapport is established with the other person you can take control of the situation and manage it as you see fit. You will be surprised how the other person will quickly follow your lead.

It is natural for human beings to fall into step with each other. After matching someone for a while you can do some things slightly different. For example, uncross your legs, scratch your nose or slow your breathing. If you have built enough rapport the other person will follow you, matching and pacing your body language.

You can apply this technique too while in an interview. By pacing the interviewers body language through mirroring how they sit and move their hands, then lead by changing your posture, the interviewer will follow you by adjusting his posture too. A more powerful example is when you match the interviewer's language patterns and build a rapport, then change your language so as to make him feel, hear or visualise what you want him to see, feel or hear.

Anchoring

This is a technique used to change state, mind or mood. It is a simple way to allow you to convert unwanted feelings to resourceful feelings in a few seconds. Creating an anchor means that you set up a stimulus response pattern to feel the way you want to, whenever you need to. The anchor can be used to stimulate calmness, for instance, and help you maintain proper confidence during the interview. The technique is reminiscent of Pavlov's dog experiments. He sounded a bell when dogs were given food. The dogs would salivate every time they observed food. After several times pairing of food with the bell, the ringing of the bell alone elicited salivation. This is known as a conditioned response.

This technique is also referred to as a biased rating of a stimulus caused by mental benchmarks or anchors that colour people's evaluation of other information. That is to say in non-technical language, the tendency to rely too heavily on one anchor or one piece of information to make a later judgment.

Anchoring are stimuli that ignite mind states, which are emotions and thoughts. For example, a certain tune may make you remember a certain person and the smell of bread can remind you of your childhood. These stimuli function automatically and mostly people are not aware of the presence of these triggers.

Before you enter into an interview you can set a personal trigger that will set off your 'best you'! This can be done by anchoring the state of confidence to a simple hand gesture. Here is how to set the anchor:

1. Step 1: Imagine a previous time in your life when you felt confident. Remember how it felt to feel confident.

2. Step 2: As your emotional state begins to automatically shift to one of self-confidence, have in your mind what hand gesture you will use to trigger that state later on when you are in the interview.

3. Step 3: Just before the peak of self-confidence happens in your mind, using your imagination and power

of recall, do the hand movement you wish to set as the anchor.

4. Step 4: Test the trigger. When you finally come back to the here and now, wait some time and then attempt to trigger off the anchored response (state of self-confidence). In addition, notice what happens.

5. Step 5: Repeat this entire process again until the anchor sticks and automatically triggers this state. When you get inside the interview, you can be sure it will work and you will appear self-confident to your interviewer.

Chapter conclusion

In this chapter, you learned a lot about NLP and some of its various techniques you can use to excel in your next job interview. Remember, however, that these are only techniques. They are meant to aid you in doing better and steer you toward the probability that you will succeed in getting the job. They are also presented as a means of giving you the upper hand over all the other candidates interviewing for the same position that you are.

AUTHOR'S FINAL NOTES

We have come to the end of the book and this has been quite some journey, has it not? There is so much to be said from the learnings in this book, especially when they are applied directly to the context of interviewing for a job you have always dreamt of. The best part comes when you actually get that job. ☺

You learnt how to differentiate yourself from the competition. You learnt how to communicate more effectively than anyone else stepping into that interview. You learnt how interviewers think and that they have been trained to detect deception and liars. You also learnt some basics of NLP, namely techniques that can be used immediately to build greater rapport with your interviewer and communicate with them in a way that leads them to believe you are in fact the best candidate for the position. What's more, you have learnt the basics of interviewing and what it takes to be an excellent interviewer and interviewee.

Will we always have bright days ahead of us? Probably not. However, when it comes to interviewing, you stand a far better chance than most people of getting the job that you want.

Overall, you cannot forget about qualifications. These factors really do determine who the best candidate for the position actually is. The best candidate relies on education, training and other things they have learned through other positions they may have held. There is so much more that goes into an individual than can be measured on a simple one or two page CV. When you get into that interview, using what you have learnt in this book, you will be able to structure your personality, style, and what you know that you have not been able necessarily to put on your CV. This means you should be able to interview well and stay aligned with the needs of that potential employer.

It is very important you do not forget this last point made. You must always align your skill set and what you know with the needs of the organisation you are aiming to join. If you cannot do this then there will be a disconnection or an incongruence that will keep you from being the best candidate. You want to make sure you are completely harmonised with the needs of the organisation and are able to represent this fit through your communication.

Remember that interviewers are just human beings and they have their and weaknesses- as we all do. They may be the decision-maker in the organisation when it comes to who gets a job and who doesn't, but when you start to look at them as just people, it's a lot easier to step into an interview and feel more confident. With the information you've learnt throughout this book you will be able to converse in a way that is eloquent and that resonates with the values of the interviewer as well as the mission and needs of the organisation.

I want to wish you well on your journey. I really do hope that you will take some time to email us after you have gotten your dream job. It is important to us that we receive your feedback because it helps us to continue measuring the results that this book brings. When it comes to making future editions of this book, we will be taking into account your recommendations and experiences from having used this information.

This book has been designed to help you be your best, most genuine and most authentic self. Our aim is to see you succeed where most fail. It is our goal that you walk away remembering what you have learnt in this book. Intentionally, this book has been made short because interviewing does not have to be a long, drawn-out or complicated experience for people. Sometimes finding a job is a full-time job. The intention of this book is to make this aspect of finding work less work for you. I hope it's helped to do this.

—Salim Shaikh

REFERENCES

Active Listening Skills for Managers. (ned). Retrieved from http://www.the-happy-manager.com/tips/active-listening-skills/

Agness, L. (2011). *Change your life with NLP: The powerful way to make your whole life better* (2nd ed.). New York: Prentice Hall Life.

Aldridge, B. (1984). *Person to person: Communicative speaking and listening skills.* New York, N.Y., USA: Oxford University Press.

Ambrester, M. L. (1997). *A rhetoric of interpersonal communication and relationships.* Bloomington, Ind: Tichenor Pub.

Basaran, K. (ned). *An important interpersonal communication skill for leadership,.*

Bauer, T., & Erdogan, B. (2010). *Organisational behaviour V1.1.* Nyack, NY: Flatworld Knowledge. (text).

Beck, R. C. (2004). *Motivation: Theories and principles* (5th ed.). Upper Saddle River, N.J: Pearson/Prentice Hall.

Beebe, S. A., & Beebe, S. J. (2012). *A concise public speaking handbook* (3rd ed.). Boston: Allyn amp; Bacon.

Bezanson, H.A. (1986). *How to successfully win job interviews: The complete guide to job interviewing* (Rev. & expanded 2nd ed.). Blaine, WA: Careers Unlimited.

Block, J. A. (2004). *Great answers! Great questions! For your job interview.* New York: McGraw-Hill.

Bowles, H., & Seedhouse, P. (Eds.). (2009). *Conversation analysis and language for specific purposes*: Vol. 63. *Linguistic insights, 1424-8689* ; (2nd ed.). New York: P. Lang.

Cairo, J. (1995). Motivation Through Giving and Receiving. In *Motivating and Goal Setting: The Keys to Achieving Success.* USA: National Press Publishers.

CASAA Listening skills. (2011). Retrieved from http://www.casaaleadership.ca/mainpages/resources/sourcebook/listening-skills.html

Cortright, S. M. (2011, March 12). *10 tips to effective & Active listening skills.* Retrieved from http://powertochange.com/students/people/listen

Courtl, and Bovee. (2012). *Business communication essentials* (5th ed.). New Jersey: Pearson Prentice Hall.

Dainton, M., & Zelley, E. D. (2005). *Applying communication theory for professional life: A practical introduction.* Thousand Oaks, Calif: SAGE Publications.

Daley, K. (1996). *Socratic selling: How to ask the questions that get the sale.* Chicago: Irwin Professional Pub.

Dessler, G., & Florida International University. (ned). *Human resource management* (FOURTEENTH EDITION ed.).

ed. (2008). *Hiring the best qualified and most talented employees: Handbook on global recruiting, screening, testing, and interviewing criteria.* Frederick, MD: Aspen.

Effective Listening Skills. (2012). Retrieved from http://www.Speechmatery.com

Erickson, M. H., & Rossi, E. L. (1979). *Hypnotherapy, an exploratory casebook.* New York: Halsted Press.

Frank, C. (2011). *Ethnographic interviewing for teacher preparation and staff development: A field guide.* New York: Teachers College Press.

Fraser, J. M. (1950). *A handbook of employment interviewing.* London: Macdonald & Evans.

Gardner, B. B., & Ph. (1944). *Case studies for interviewing methods and techniques, Business 245, the University of Chicago.* Chicago, Ill: The University of Chicago Bookstore.

Gershon, D., & Straub, G. (2011). *Empowerment: The art of creating your life as you want it* (2nd ed.). New York: Sterling Pub.

Hanna, S. L. (2009). *Career by design: Communicating your way to success* (4th ed.). Upper Saddle River, N.J: Pearson Prentice Hall.

Hansen, K. (2012). *Behavioral Job Interviewing Strategies for Job-Seekers.* Retrieved from http://www.quintcareers.com/behavioral_interviewing.html

Harris, T. E. (2002). *Applied organisational communication: Principles and pragmatics for future practice* (2nd ed.). Mahwah, N.J: Lawrence Erlbaum Associates.

Henk, T. (2005). *Communication in organisations: Basic skills and conversation models*. New York, NY: Psychology Press.

Hoffman, B. (1999). *Cold reading and how to be good at it*. Rancho Mirage, CA: Dramaline.

Hybels, S., & Weaver, R. L., II. (2012). *Communicating effectively*. New York: McGraw-Hill.

Ivey, A. (2010). *Intentional interviewing ; Counselling: Facilitating client development in a multicultural society* (7th Ed.). Belmont, CA: Brooks/Cole.

Krieger, S. H., & Neumann, R. K., Jr. (2011). *Essential lawyering skills: Interviewing, counselling & negotiation, and persuasive fact analysis* (4th Ed.). New York, NY: Aspen Publishers.

Ledochowski, I. (2003). *The deep trance training manual*. Carmarthen, Wales ; Williston, VT: Crown House Pub.

Martin John Yate. (1987). *Hiring the best: A manager's guide to effective interviewing*. Boston: B. Adams.

Matsumoto, D. (Ed.). (2010). *APA handbook of interpersonal communication*. New York: Walter de Gruyter.

McClam, T., & Woodside, M. (2010). *Initial interviewing: What students want to know*. Belmont, CA: Brooks/Cole.

Miller, K., National Centre for Health Statistics, Willson, S., National Centre for Health Statistics, Chepp, V., & Centre, N. (ned). *Cognitive interviewing methodology*.

Miller. (2003). *An Overview of Motivational Interviewing.* New York, NY: The Guilford Press. Retrieved from http://www.motivationalinterview.org/quick_links/about_mi.html

Personal Goal Setting. (2014). Retrieved from http://www.mindtools.com/page6.html

Pfeffer, J., & Sutton, R. I. (2000). *The knowing-doing gap: How smart companies turn knowledge into action.* Boston, Mass: Harvard Business School Press.

Quintessentialcareers.com. (2010). *Informational Interviewing Tutorial.* Kettle Falls: Quintessential Careers. Retrieved from http://www.quintcareers.com/information_background.html

Sanchez, M. (ned). *8 Strategies for Achieving Smart Goals.* Retrieved from http://www.projectsmart.co.uk/8-strategies-for-achieving-smart-goals.html

Skills You Need. (unknown). *Active Listening.* Retrieved from http://www.skillsyouneed.com/ips/active-listening.html

Susan Britton Whitcomb. (2008). *Interview magic: Job interview secrets from America's career and life coach* (2nd ed.). Indianapolis: JIST.

Thomas, W. (2005). *Career Mechanics.* Washington, DC: Bramor Career Pub.

Washington Department of Financial Institutions. (ned). *How to save money while unemployed.* Retrieved from http://dfi.wa.gov/financial-education/job-loss-resources.htm

Wasserman, N. (2000, March 1). *A closer look at behaviour based interviewing.* Retrieved from http://www.inc.com/articles/2000/03/17957.html

Yate, M. (1990). *Hiring the best: How to staff your department right the first time* (3rd ed.). Holbrook, Mass: B. Adams.

ABOUT THE AUTHOR

Salim Shaikh is the owner of both Smartlyte Limited and CV Assistant (UK & UAE). He provides training, coaching and consultancy for the employment market.

With over 2 decade's worth of experience, Salim is considered an expert in the field of career development. He has conducted over 300 workshops on a range of employment issues, from pre employment programmes for the long term unemployed, to coaching businesses on improving staff retention. His success lies in transforming individuals to discover their true potential and is recognised throughout the UK and internationally.

After giving in to the demands of friends, family and colleagues, Salim has collated his best tips and advice into a short book.

www.ingramcontent.com/pod-product-compliance
Lightning Source LLC
Chambersburg PA
CBHW021015180526
45163CB00005B/1957